MW01047560

BOARDS, SKIS & SKATES

MARY ELIZABETH SALZMANN

Consulting Editor, Diane Craig, M.A./Reading Specialist

A Division of ABDO

ABDO
Publishing Company

visit us at www.abdopublishing.com

Published by ABDO Publishing Company, a division of ABDO, P.O. Box 398166, Minneapolis, Minnesota 55439. Copyright © 2012 by Abdo Consulting Group, Inc. International copyrights reserved in all countries. No part of this book may be reproduced in any form without written permission from the publisher. SandCastle™ is a trademark and logo of ABDO Publishing Company.

Printed in the United States of America, North Mankato, Minnesota
062011
092011

 PRINTED ON RECYCLED PAPER

Editor: Katherine Hengel
Content Developer: Nancy Tuminelly
Design and Production: Anders Hanson
Photo Credits: Thinkstock (Thomas Northcut, Comstock, Hemera Technologies, Stockbyte), Shutterstock

Library of Congress Cataloging-in-Publication Data
Salzmann, Mary Elizabeth, 1968-
  Boards, skis & skates / Mary Elizabeth Salzmann.
    p. cm. -- (Sports gear)
  ISBN 978-1-61714-824-8
  1. Sporting goods--Juvenile literature. 2. Winter sports--Juvenile literature. I. Title.
  GV745.S343 2012
  688.7´6--dc22
                    2010053048

SANDCASTLE™ LEVEL: FLUENT

SandCastle™ books are created by a team of professional educators, reading specialists, and content developers around five essential components—phonemic awareness, phonics, vocabulary, text comprehension, and fluency—to assist young readers as they develop reading skills and strategies and increase their general knowledge. All books are written, reviewed, and leveled for guided reading, early reading intervention, and Accelerated Reader® programs for use in shared, guided, and independent reading and writing activities to support a balanced approach to literacy instruction. The SandCastle™ series has four levels that correspond to early literacy development. The levels are provided to help teachers and parents select appropriate books for young readers.

Emerging Readers
(no flags)

Beginning Readers
(1 flag)

Transitional Readers
(2 flags)

Fluent Readers
(3 flags)

CONTENTS

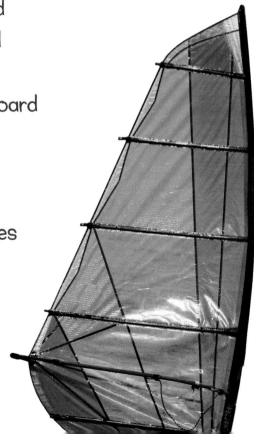

What Are...

BOARDS, SKIS & SKATES ?

Boards, skis, and skates are sports gear.

4

Athletes use them to move! They go over the ground, snow, ice, or water.

SKATEBOARD

A skateboard is a board with four wheels.

Skateboarding was an event in the first X-Games in 1995.

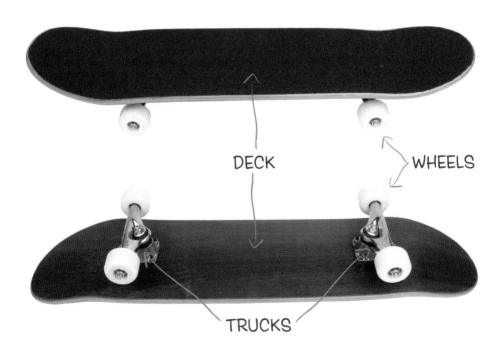

DECK

WHEELS

TRUCKS

Some skateboarders do jumps and tricks on their boards.

SNOWBOARD

A snowboard is a long board used on the snow.

TAIL

BINDINGS

WAIST

NOSE

The first snowboard was called the Snurfer.

Snowboards are used on snowy hills. They are great for jumps and tricks!

SURFBOARD

A surfboard is a long, oval board.

There are three kinds of surfboards. There are longboards, shortboards, and bodyboards.

BODYBOARD

SHORTBOARD

LONGBOARD

Surfboards are used to ride waves.

WINDSURF BOARD

SAIL

A windsurf board has a **sail**. The wind pushes it across the water.

MAST

BOW

FOOT STRAPS

STERN

12

Some windsurfers can do jumps and spins!

SNOW SKIS

Snow skis are long and flat.

DOWNHILL SKIS

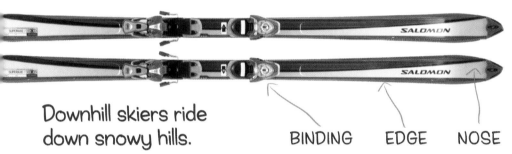

Downhill skiers ride down snowy hills.

BINDING   EDGE   NOSE

CROSS-COUNTRY SKIS

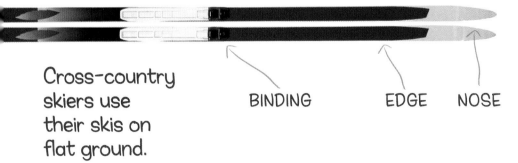

Cross-country skiers use their skis on flat ground.

BINDING   EDGE   NOSE

Ski jumpers ride down hills with **ramps** at the bottom. The ramp makes them fly into the air.

WATER SKIS

Water skis are long,
flat boards used
on water.

TIP

BINDING

TAIL

TOW ROPE

The skier holds a rope. The rope connects to the back of a boat. The boat pulls the skier across the water.

ICE SKATES

Ice skates are boots that have metal blades on the bottom.

TOE PICK

Ice hockey players wear hockey skates.

Figure skates have a toe pick. It's on the front of each blade. The toe picks help the skater spin and jump.

Speed skates are used for racing.

ROLLER SKATES

Roller skates are boots that have wheels!

A quad skate has four wheels.

WHEELS

TOE STOP

An inline skate can have three, four, or five wheels. The wheels are set in a line.

FUN FACTS

- The surfboard was invented in Hawaii.

- Ice skates were invented in Finland about 5,000 years ago.

- There is a National Museum of Roller Skating in Nebraska.

QUICK QUIZ

1. Boards, skis, and skates are not sports gear. True or False?

2. A skateboard has four wheels. True or False?

3. Figure skates have a toe pick. True or False?

4. Most inline skates have ten or more wheels. True or False?

GLOSSARY

athlete – someone who is good at sports or games that require strength, speed, or agility.

connect - to join two or more things together.

oval - having a shape much like an egg.

ramp – a lane or path that slopes up or down.

sail - a large, strong cloth that catches the wind.